I0814791

General Thomas Gage

ICONIC AMERICA

12 ICONIC AMERICAN BATTLES

BLACK RABBIT BOOKS

MARNE VENTURA

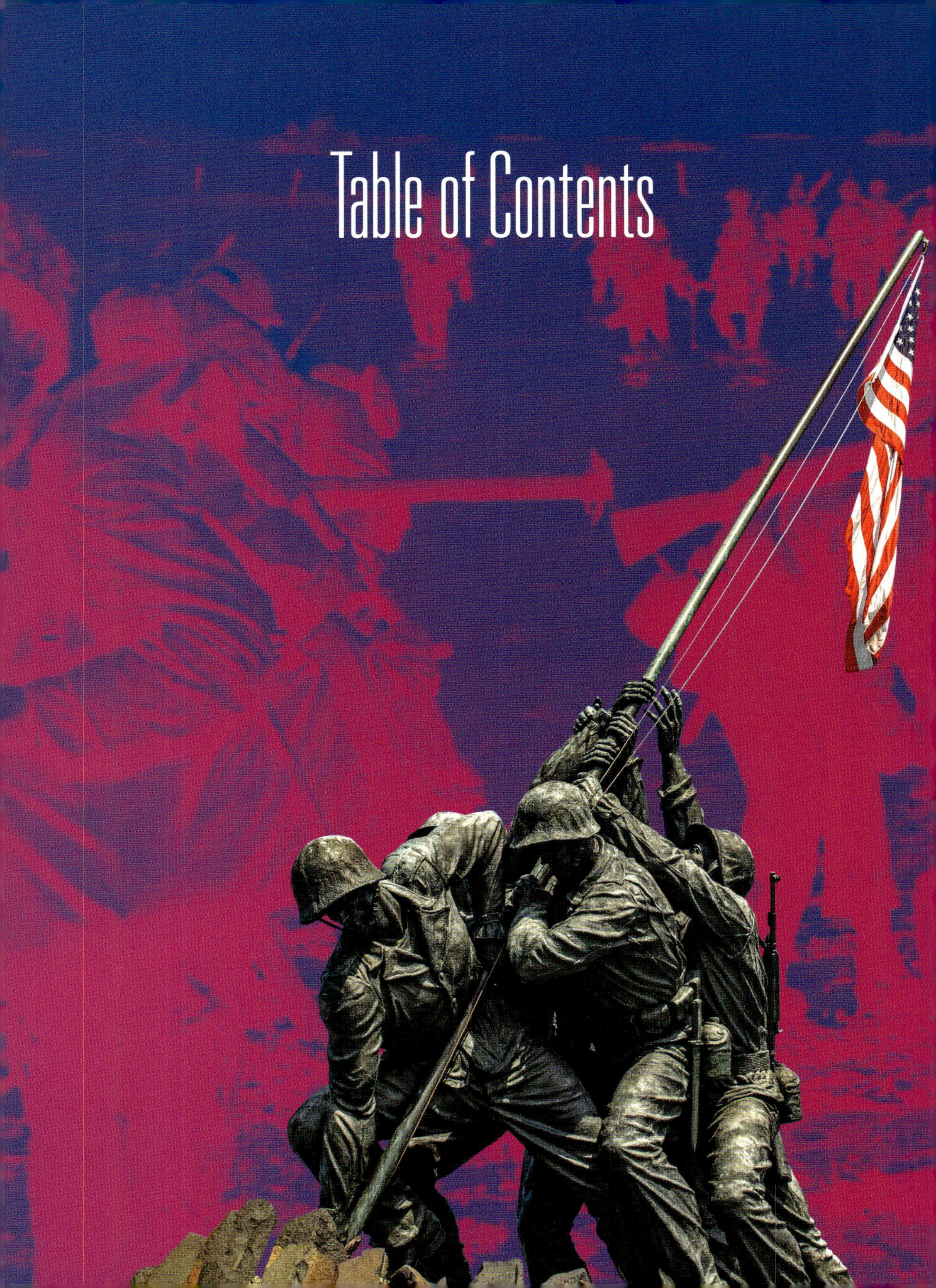

Table of Contents

American Revolution Starts with Battles of *Lexington and Concord*

1

American history is full of iconic battles. Two of them began America's fight to become a country. In 1775, American **colonies** were under the rule of Great Britain. Many colonists wanted to be independent. They gathered weapons for a **rebellion**. One stash was in Concord, Massachusetts. Britain sent General Thomas Gage and 700 soldiers to this **colony**. They planned to destroy the weapons. They wanted to stop the **uprising**.

A reenactor shows weapons a colonial soldier would have used.

The British soldiers arrived in Lexington, Massachusetts, on April 19, 1775. The "redcoats" found 77 colonial soldiers waiting for them. The two sides faced off across the town square. A shot was fired. It is not clear who fired it. Then both sides began firing. Moments later, eight colonists were dead. Ten more were wounded.

The British marched about 7 miles (11 kilometers) to Concord. They searched for guns and supplies. But the colonists had been warned. They had already moved most of their stash. Meanwhile, hundreds of colonist soldiers arrived. They rushed the British. The fighting was over quickly. The British fell back to Boston. Colonial soldiers kept up the fight. They hid behind trees, rocks, and homes. They killed or wounded many British soldiers.

These two battles marked the start of the Revolutionary War. They showed that the colonists could stand up against the British force. This inspired many colonists to join the war.

273 British casualties at both Lexington and Concord.

There were about 300 to 400 colonists in Concord. • The colonists lost 95 soldiers in all. • Within months, thousands of colonists joined the Continental Army.

The battles at Lexington and Concord inspired more men to join the fight for independence.

Colonists Fight Fiercely *at Bunker Hill*

2

Bayonets attached to the end of rifles for up-close fighting.

Not all iconic battles were won. Sometimes a battle becomes a legend because it sends a new message. This is what happened at Bunker Hill. This hill is across the bay from Boston. It was a good military position. Early in the Revolutionary War, the British planned to take control of it. The colonists heard of the plan. They set out to take control first. They traveled in the dark. They passed Bunker Hill and set up on Breed's Hill, the next hill over.

On June 17, 1775, the British sent their troops to take the hill. The redcoats rushed up with their **bayonets**. The colonial soldiers hid in trenches and behind walls. They shot at British soldiers. More British soldiers charged the hill. The colonists ran out of **ammunition**. They fought with clubs, fists, and rocks. Finally, the British forced them to flee.

Right: US stamp of Bunker Hill Monument in Boston.

Below: A painting shows the moment when the British overran the colonists, forcing them to retreat.

The colonists lost the battle, but they fought fiercely. The British ended up with more damage than the colonists. Historians say this was a turning point in the war. It was the first major battle of the American Revolution. The colonists proved they could hold up against the mighty British army. This gave Americans the confidence to keep fighting.

3 Number of times the British troops charged up Breed's Hill.

About 1,200 colonial soldiers fought against 2,100 British troops. • The colonists lost 411 soldiers. • More than 1,000 British soldiers were killed or wounded.

WHICH HILL? The battle is named after Bunker Hill. But the battle actually took place on Breed's Hill. This was a smaller, lower hill. The Americans thought it was a more threatening position. It was closer to Boston and the British forces. Later, the British army made a map of the battle. They labeled Breed's Hill as Bunker Hill. Over time, the name stuck.

A monument honors the Battle of Bunker Hill in Boston, Massachusetts.

Battle of Saratoga Turns the Tide *of the Revolution*

3

It was the third year of the American Revolution. British General John Burgoyne pushed his army toward Albany, New York. The British hoped to cut off New England from the other colonies. American troops under General Horatio Gates stood in Burgoyne's way.

On September 19, 1777, drums signaled the British attack. The American troops were ready. The armies met at Freeman's Farm near Saratoga, New York. The soldiers fought all day. As night came, the colonists fell back.

General Horatio Gates

On October 7, Burgoyne attacked again. Gates had set up cannons on the highest hill. It was called Bemis Heights. By day's end, many British soldiers had died. Their supplies ran low. The 5,000 remaining British troops fell back to Saratoga. About 20,000 American troops surrounded the British forces there. Burgoyne was outnumbered. He surrendered on October 17.

The Battle of Saratoga was a major victory for the colonies. It was another turning point in the war. While the British army continued to fight in the South, American troops felt hope that they could win. Partly due to the win, France decided to support the American side.

FRANCE'S HELP

France and Britain were enemies before and during the American Revolution. They competed for territory and power. France helped America win the war. They loaned America money. They sent supplies, ships, and soldiers. France hoped to gain more territory and power if Britain was defeated.

8,000 Number of British troops who marched to Albany, New York.

The American army grew from 12,000 to 20,000 as more men arrived. • Fighting took place at Freeman's Farm, Bemis Heights, and Saratoga. • The American win was a turning point in the war.

General Burgoyne surrendered his sword to General Gates after the battle.

4 Siege of Yorktown Ends *American Revolution*

The colonists had been fighting the British for independence for six years. British General Charles Cornwallis led his troops to Yorktown, Virginia. From there, they could take over nearby towns. They could also wait there for British supply ships. But General George Washington chose to block him. He marched his men to Yorktown. French troops joined them.

On September 28, 1781, the American and French armies arrived. They dug trenches around the British army. They worked day and night. Troops poured into the trenches. They brought cannons with them. George Washington fired the first cannon. The Americans' attack lasted for three weeks.

Cannons were used to blow holes in the enemy's ranks.

Cornwallis saw that the British were outnumbered. They tried to escape

Cornwallis surrendered to Washington after the Battle of Yorktown.

28,900 Total number of soldiers at Yorktown.

About 19,900 American troops outnumber 9,000 British troops. • 8,589 British and 389 American troops died. • The trench around Yorktown was more than 1 mile (1.6 km) long.

An art piece shows how hard American and British soldiers fought at Yorktown.

across the river to New Jersey. A bad storm made them turn their boats back. Then French ships arrived. The French trapped the British navy. Cornwallis's men could not escape by sea. The British army had no way out. The American and French troops hammered the British troops with cannon fire. On October 19, 1781, Cornwallis sent an officer to surrender.

The Battle of Yorktown marked the end of the war. The American colonists won. The United States of America became a new nation.

Think About It

How might the world be different if the British had won the Revolutionary War?

Texans Fight for Independence *at the Alamo*

5

In 1836, Texas was ruled by Mexico. Texans wanted to rule themselves. They were ready to fight for independence. About 200 Texans took over the Alamo. It was a former **mission** and military fort in San Antonio. Several thousand Mexican soldiers arrived on February 23, 1836. They attacked the Alamo. The Mexicans wanted to take back control of San Antonio.

For 12 days, the Texans held off the Mexican army. The Mexicans shot cannons at the Alamo's walls. The Texans fired back with **muskets**, rifles, and cannons. They forced the Mexican army back. But the Texans were outnumbered. More help never came.

On March 6, 1836, Mexican General Antonio López de Santa Anna gave the signal to strike. The Mexican army rushed in. Soon, gun shots

A plate at the Alamo honors the men who died in the battle.

and yelling filled the air. The Texans fought with rifles, knives, and their bare hands. They would not give up. But the Mexican army won. Almost all the Texans were killed within two hours. "Remember the Alamo" became a battle cry for Texans.

The Alamo was a tragic loss for Texans. But it was a symbol of how hard they were willing to fight for independence. Texas won independence six weeks later at the Battle of San Jacinto.

A painting shows how hard the Texans fought against the Mexicans.

Many people visit the Alamo Mission in San Antonio, Texas, to learn about the famous battle.

12 Days the Alamo was under **siege**.

Davy Crockett, a famous frontiersman, fought and died at the Alamo. • Between 1,800 and 6,000 Mexican troops fought at the Alamo. • Between 600 and 1,600 Mexicans were killed in the battle.

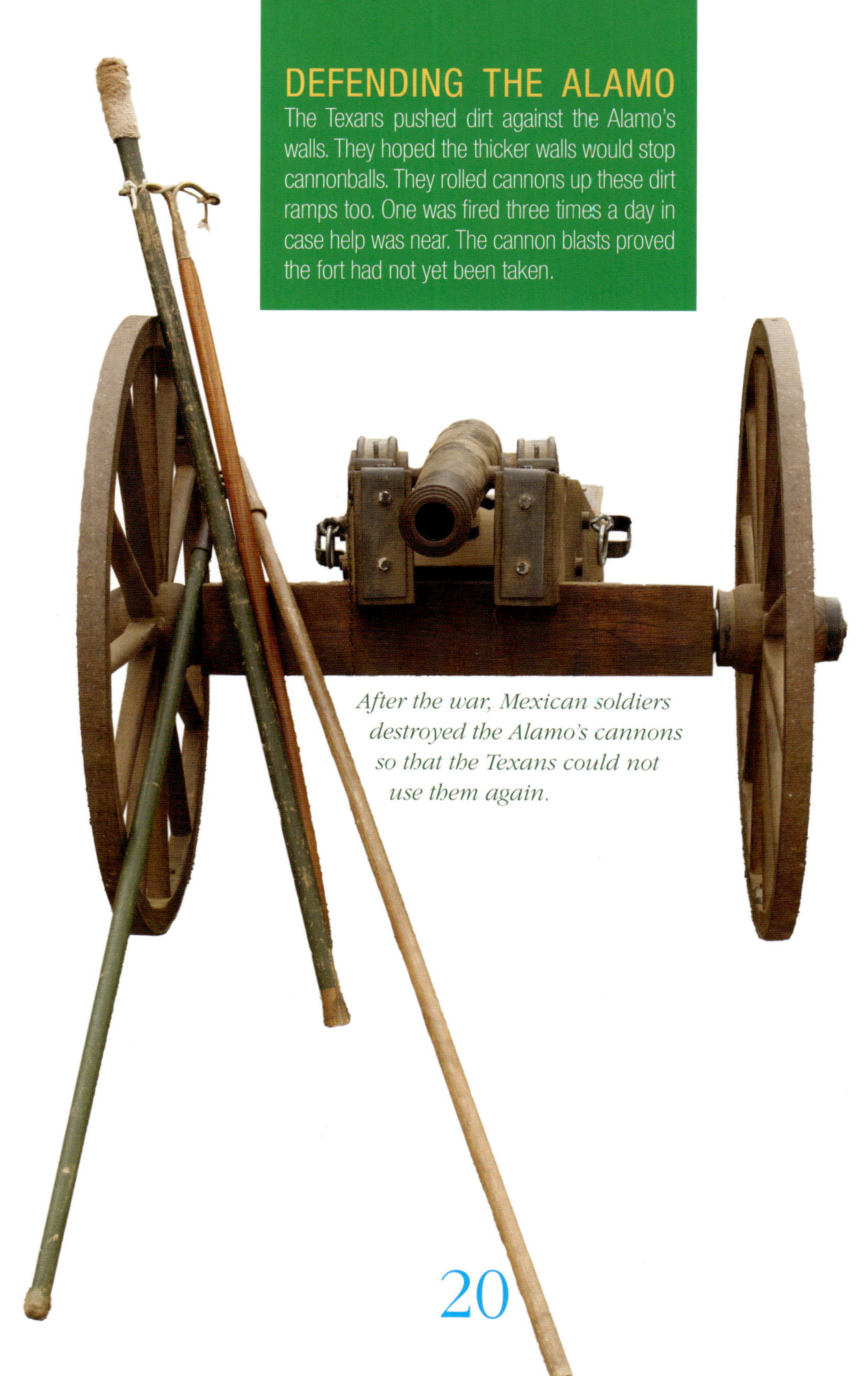

DEFENDING THE ALAMO

The Texans pushed dirt against the Alamo's walls. They hoped the thicker walls would stop cannonballs. They rolled cannons up these dirt ramps too. One was fired three times a day in case help was near. The cannon blasts proved the fort had not yet been taken.

After the war, Mexican soldiers destroyed the Alamo's cannons so that the Texans could not use them again.

Union Wins Bloody Victory in *Battle of Antietam*

6

The American Civil War was fought from 1861 to 1865. The war began because states disagreed about banning slavery. The Union army fought for the North. The Confederate Army fought for the South.

A year into the war, Confederate General Robert E. Lee led his army north. At this point in the war, most of the battles had been fought in the South. Lee wanted to push his forces into the northern states. Then, they could possibly take Washington, DC.

General Robert E. Lee

Lee stopped near Antietam Creek by Sharpsburg, Maryland. He planned to attack the Union army. Union General Joseph Hooker and his army arrived. The fighting began. It went on for many hours. Almost 2,000 Confederate fighters were trapped and killed. The spot became known as Bloody Lane. The day ended with 13,724 Confederate and 12,410 Union casualties. The next day, General Lee fell back to Virginia.

The Battle at Antietam was the deadliest one-day battle in US history. President Lincoln called it a win for the Union. On September 22, 1862, he read a draft of the **Emancipation** Proclamation. This was a vow to free the slaves. It went into effect January 1, 1863.

Union troops rush across one of the creek's bridges to push back the Confederates.

26,134 Total number of troops on both sides who were killed, wounded, or listed as missing.

The battle was fought near a branch of the Potomac River. • About 60,000 soldiers fought for the Union. • About 30,000 soldiers fought for the Confederacy.

Bloody Lane is part of a national park where visitors can learn about America's bloodiest battle.

Battle of Gettysburg Stops *Confederate Invasion*

7

By the summer of 1863, the US Civil War had been raging for more than two years. General Robert E. Lee once again set out to invade the North. He hoped to defeat the Union. His army entered Pennsylvania. They met Union troops at Gettysburg on July 1, 1863. For two days, the two armies fought. Wave after wave of attacks caused many deaths on both sides.

By July 3, 1863, only 1 mile (1.6 km) of open field separated the two sides. That morning, the Union stopped firing their cannons. They hoped to trick the Confederates into coming out into the open. The plan worked. General Lee thought the Union's cannons had been wiped out. He ordered his men to charge the center of the line. Major General George Pickett led the charge.

Think About It

Look up the Gettysburg Address. President Lincoln delivered it four months after the Battle of Gettysburg. What message did it declare? How does it relate to the battle?

About 13,000 troops rushed across the open field. Bullets zipped through the wheat. The Union fired their cannons again. More than half of Pickett's troops died. Lee's plan had failed. His soldiers were worn out. They returned to Virginia. They ended their invasion of the North.

The Battle of Gettysburg was a turning point in the Civil War. More soldiers died there than in any other battle. The Confederacy lost hope of winning the war.

Actors fill in the Confederacy lines during a reenactment of the Battle of Gettysburg.

Custer Defeated at Battle of *Little Bighorn*

8

In 1868, a treaty granted land west of the Missouri River to Native Americans. These included the Lakota, Cheyenne, and Arapaho peoples. But white miners searching for gold wanted the land. The US government ordered the Lakota to move to **reservations** by 1876. The Lakota said no. The government sent troops.

Lieutenant Colonel George Custer was in charge of the 7th **Cavalry**. His troops searched for camps on the Little Bighorn River. On the morning of June 25, 1876, Custer's **scouts** found a Lakota/Cheyenne village. About 6,000 people were camped there.

Lieutenant Colonel George Custer

Custer split up his cavalry. He planned to attack from all sides. Major Marcus Reno's troops reached the camp first. The Cheyenne and Lakota warriors were surprised. They ran for their guns. They leapt

Lt Col Custer rides into battle on horseback with his troops.

onto horses. They shot back at the soldiers. Reno fell back. He joined troops led by Captain Frederick Benteen. At the same time, Custer and his troops moved to the far side of camp. As Reno fell back, the warriors attacked Custer's men. The US troops were outnumbered. Custer and all his men were killed within an hour. After the defeat, the US government flooded the area with troops. The Lakota and Cheyenne peoples were forced to give up.

210 Men led into battle by Custer, all of whom were killed.

Of the 390 troops led by other US commanders, 53 were killed and 52 wounded. • US troops faced about 2,000 Cheyenne and Lakota warriors. • About 30 Lakota and Cheyenne warriors were killed in battle. So were several women and children.

VISION OF VICTORY

A few weeks before the battle, Chief Sitting Bull (left) held a ceremony. It was called the Sun Dance. Sitting Bull danced, sang, and prayed. He had a vision of soldiers falling into the camp upside down. The Lakota thought this vision meant they were going to win a big battle soon.

Japan Launches Surprise Attack *on Pearl Harbor*

9

Pearl Harbor is a bay on the coast of Oahu island in Hawaii. The US built a naval base there in the early 1900s. It was used during wars.

In 1939, World War II began. It was a fight between the Allies and the Axis powers. The Allies were the United Kingdom, the Soviet Union, and China. The Axis powers were Nazi Germany, Italy, and Japan. The US had not joined the war. But they supported the Allies. In 1941, they stopped doing business with Japan. Japan wanted to take over the South Pacific. Pearl Harbor was a threat to Japan's plan.

Newspapers around the country printed stories about the attack at Oahu, Hawaii.

Honolulu Star-Bulletin 1st EXTRA

(Associated Press by Transpacific Telephone)

SAN FRANCISCO, Dec. 7.—President Roosevelt announced this morning that Japanese planes had attacked Manila and Pearl Harbor.

WAR!

OAHU BOMBED BY JAPANESE PLANES

SIX KNOWN DEAD, 21 INJURED, AT EMERGENCY HOSPITAL

Attack Made On Island's Defense Areas

Hundreds See City Bombed

Names of Dead and Injured

Schools Closed

Editorial

On December 7, 1941, Japanese planes made a surprise attack on the US naval base at Pearl Harbor.

They sank and destroyed battleships. They wrecked 180 aircraft. More than 2,300 Americans were killed.

The attack on Pearl Harbor caused the United States to declare war on Japan. Three days later, Germany and Italy declared war on the United States. America was now fighting in World War II. They were one of the Allies.

A naval photo shows the destruction of the USS Arizona *after the attack on Pearl Harbor.*

8 US battleships damaged in the raid. Six were repaired and returned to service.

The attack started at 7:55 a.m. • The attack lasted one hour and fifteen minutes. • There were fewer than 100 Japanese casualties.

A Japanese bomber flies over the naval base at Pearl Harbor.

Think About It President Franklin Roosevelt called the Pearl Harbor attack "a day which will live in infamy." What do you think he meant? What are some other dates in history that could be described this way?.

Battle of Midway Is a Turning Point *in World War II*

10

A Japanese fighter jet (top) flies near a US bomber in a recreation of the Battle of Midway.

The Midway Islands are in the central Pacific Ocean. In 1940, the US Navy built an air base there. By 1942, the United States was fighting in World War II. The Japanese were fighting against the United States. The Japanese wanted to destroy the US naval fleet in the Pacific. From there they could strike Hawaii again. But Americans had unlocked a code the Japanese used to make their plans. Three US aircraft carriers were waiting for them at Midway Island.

On June 4, 1942, about 90 Japanese planes attacked. The United States returned fire from the ground. American planes took off. But the Japanese planes were new and fast. They shot down the old American planes. Then the Japanese had to return to their aircraft carriers for more fuel. The next wave of US bombers surprised the Japanese. In minutes, three Japanese

150 Number of US planes that were destroyed. More than 300 Japanese aircraft were destroyed.

The battle took place mostly in the air. • Japan lost most of its aircraft carriers and its best pilots. • One US aircraft carrier was destroyed. Japan lost four carriers.

CODE BREAKER Joe Rochefort worked for US intelligence. He cracked the Japanese naval code. Rochefort figured out that the Japanese military called Midway "AF." He heard them talking about plans to attack AF. Rochefort warned the US Navy so they could be ready.

carriers went up in flames. Americans downed the last carrier the next day. More than 3,000 Japanese troops died.

The Battle of Midway was a big win for the Allies. It changed the course of WWII. Before the battle, Japan planned to invade the Pacific Islands. Their loss at Midway put an end to this plan.

Smoke from burning oil tanks fills the air on the second day of the Battle of Midway.

Allies Free France with Invasion *of Normandy*

11

World War II started September 1, 1939. By 1940, Germany had taken control of France. The Allied forces wanted to free France from Axis power. In June 1944, US troops planned to **storm** the beaches of Normandy, France. Canadian and British troops would join them. On the night of June 6, thousands of Allied soldiers dropped by parachute from planes. They landed inland from the beaches in Normandy.

Axis obstacles made landing on the beaches of Normandy more difficult and dangerous.

Earlier that day, a huge fleet of Allied ships left England for France. When they got to Normandy, thousands of troops were carried to shore in small boats. The waters were full of mines. Vehicles called minesweepers cleared a path to the beach. Under heavy fire, the Allied troops jumped into the water and ran for the beach. The fighting at Omaha Beach was brutal. American troops faced steep cliffs and bluffs. German soldiers fired at them from hidden bunkers. The Americans moved forward. They took out the German guns. They broke through the German lines.

The invasion of Normandy was also known as D-Day. It was a big win for the Allies. By the end of August 1944, Allied troops had freed France and were moving into Nazi Germany.

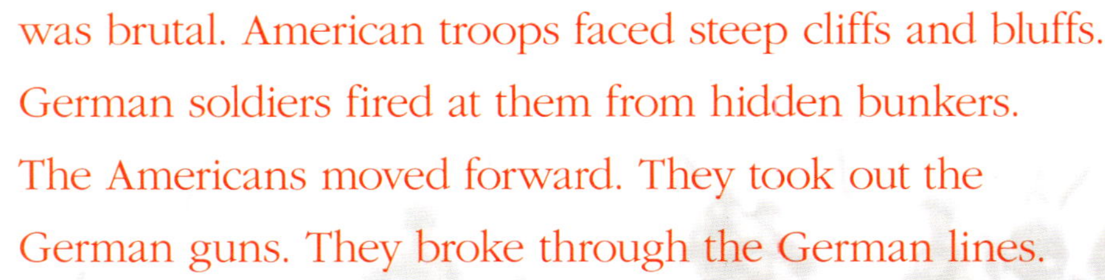

GHOST ARMY The Allies tricked the Germans. They set up fake army camps on a different beach. The camps had dummy tanks, jeeps, and aircraft. Sound effects made them seem real. Planes dropped dolls with parachutes. Each blew up when it neared the ground. Germans thought the Allied forces were attacking on the wrong beach.

Allied soldiers storm the beaches at Normandy on D-Day.

2,501 Americans killed on the first day of battle.

The invasion of Normandy was officially called Operation Overlord. • There were about 156,115 Allied troops who landed in Normandy. • They stormed five beaches.

US Captures Military Base *at Iwo Jima*

12 The island of Iwo Jima is southeast of Japan. In 1945, the island was ruled by Japan. The United States wanted control of the island. It would make a good base for fighter planes during World War II.

On February 19, 1945, US Marines landed on Iwo Jima. The Japanese did not strike right away. They were hiding underground. They had set up bunkers in the island's caves. They waited there to strike. More Marines landed. Finally, the Japanese struck. Soon, the beaches were covered in damaged equipment and wounded soldiers.

For 36 days, the battle raged. Marines cleared out one bunker at a time. The Japanese troops used secret tunnels. They snuck back into old bunkers. On March 26, 1945, the United States took control

War vehicles lie smashed by Japanese weapons on the black sands of Iwo Jima.

of the island. It was one of the bloodiest battles in Marine Corps history.

After the battle, the United States continued to bomb Japan. It used Iwo Jima as a base. US control of the island helped the Allies win World War II. It was a landing site for bombers. Future air raids against Japan helped end the war.

A famous photo shows a Marine still clutching his gun after a Japanese sniper attack at Iwo Jima.

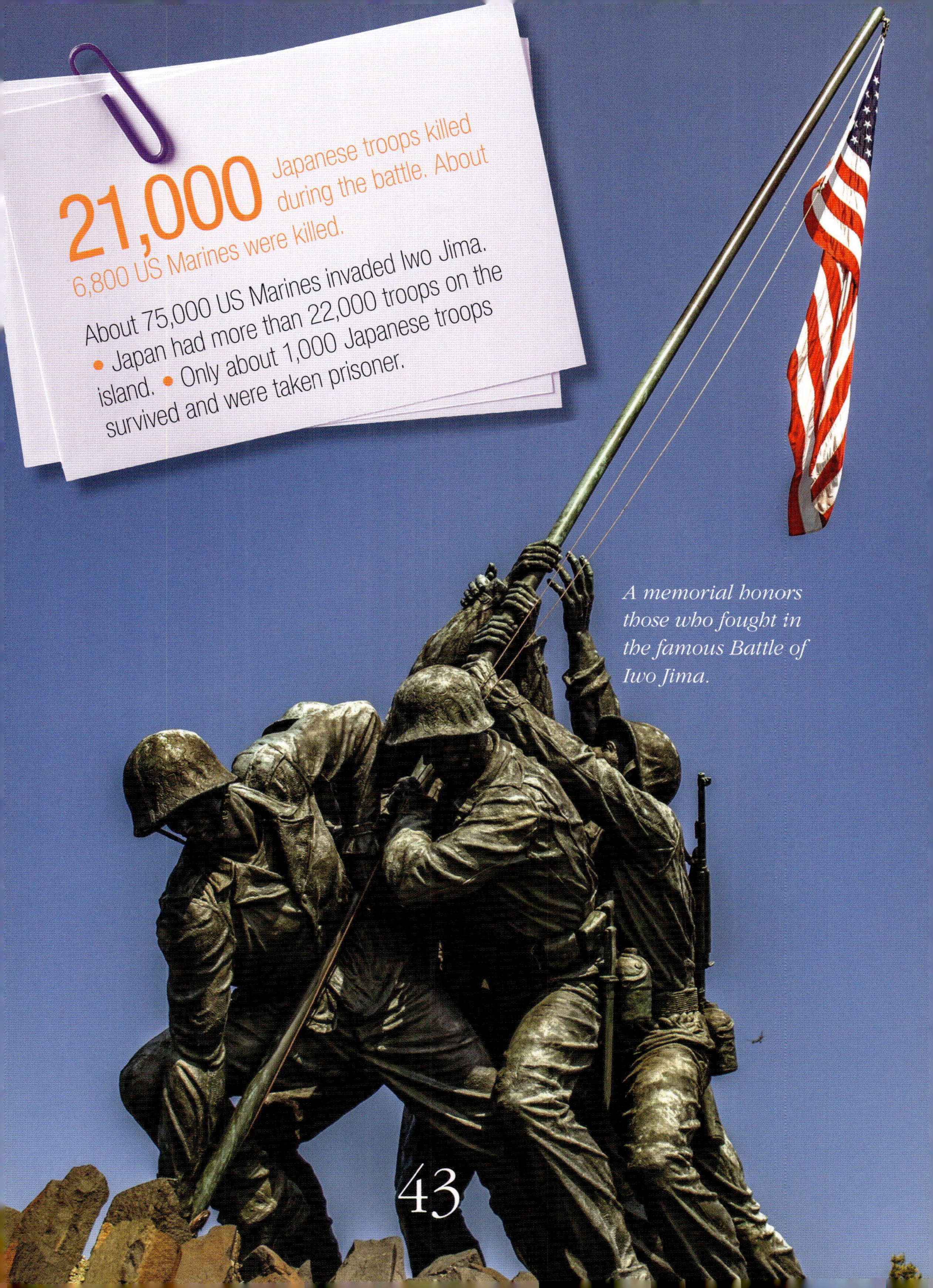

21,000 Japanese troops killed during the battle. About 6,800 US Marines were killed.

About 75,000 US Marines invaded Iwo Jima. • Japan had more than 22,000 troops on the island. • Only about 1,000 Japanese troops survived and were taken prisoner.

A memorial honors those who fought in the famous Battle of Iwo Jima.

Where in the World?

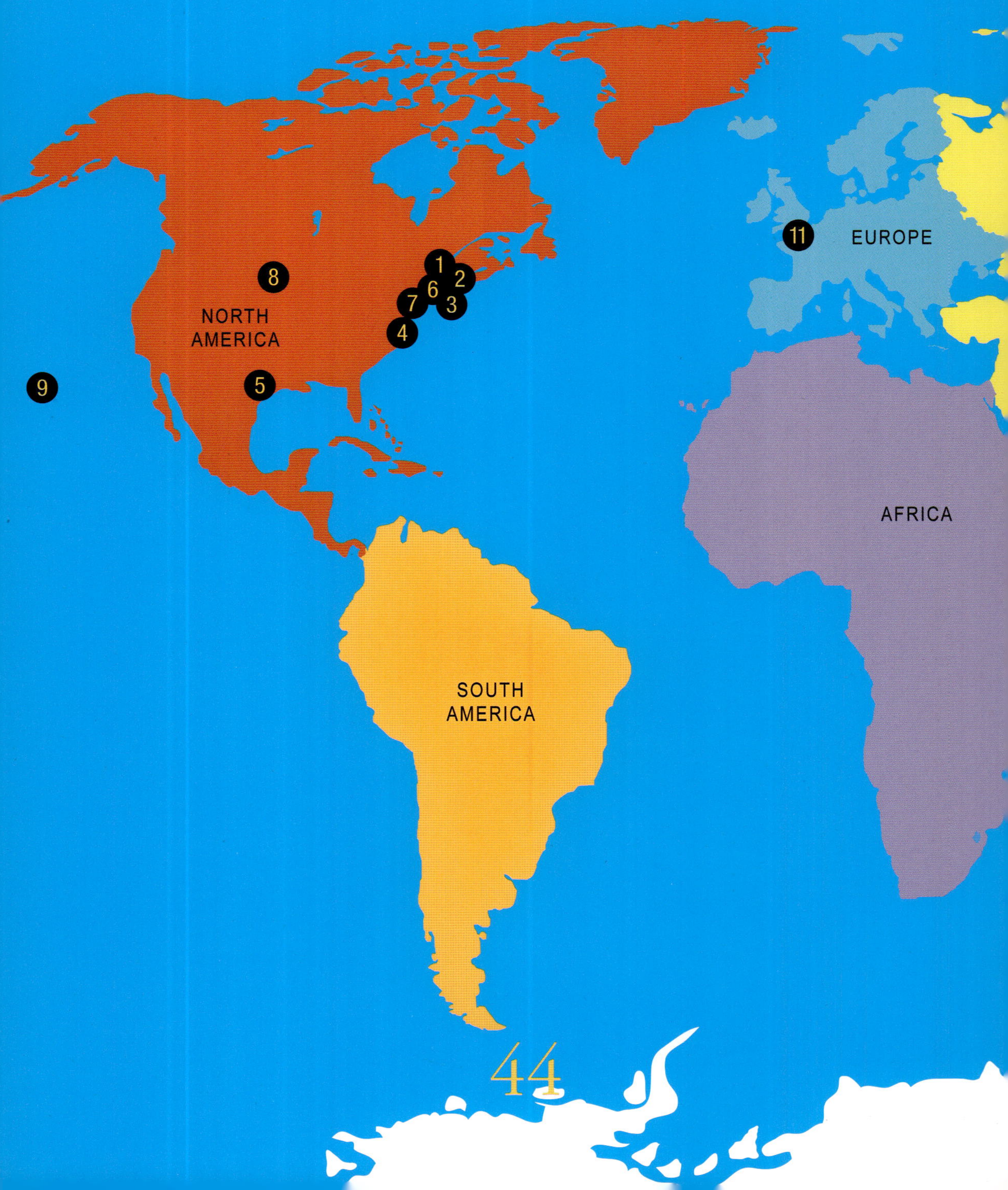

1 **Battles of Lexington and Concord**
Lexington and Concord, Massachusetts

2 **Battle of Bunker Hill**
Boston, Massachusetts

3 **Battle of Saratoga**
Stillwater, New York

4 **Siege of Yorktown**
Yorktown, Virginia

5 **Battle of the Alamo**
San Antonio, Texas

6 **Battle of Antietam**
Sharpsburg, Maryland

7 **Battle of Gettysburg**
Gettysburg, Pennsylvania

8 **Battle of Little Bighorn**
near Little Bighorn River

9 **Attack on Pearl Harbor**
Oahu, Hawaii

10 **Battle of Midway**
Midway Atoll

11 **Invasion of Normandy**
Normandy, France

12 **Battle of Iwo Jima**
Iwo Jima, Japan

Glossary

ammunition
An object that is shot from a weapon.

bayonet
A long knife attached to the end of a rifle.

casualty
A military person lost through death, wounds, illness, enemy capture, or goes missing.

colony
An area that is controlled by another country.

emancipation
The act of freeing someone from someone else's control.

mission
A group of buildings where people sent by the Spanish church lived and worked.

musket
A long gun popular during the 1700s and 1800s.

rebellion
An effort by many people to change the government or leader of a country by the use of protest or violence.

reservation
An area of land that the US government set aside as a place for Native Americans to live.

scout
Member of an army whose job it is to collect information.

siege
When an armed force surrounds a building or army until it surrenders.

storm
To attack and capture a place suddenly by using a lot of force or a large number of people.

uprising
A usually violent effort by many people to change the government or leader of a country; another name for rebellion.

For More Information

Books

Cooke, Tim. *Surprise Attack!: Pearl Harbor, 1941*. Minneapolis: Bearport Publishing, 2023.

Levy, Janey. *The Alamo*. New York: Gareth Stevens Publishing, 2025.

Wilberforce, Bert. *The American Revolution*. Buffalo, NY: Cavendish Square Publishing, 2024.

Websites

The Battle of the Alamo
www.ducksters.com/history/us_1800s/battle_of_the_alamo.php

Defining Battles of the Civil War
education.nationalgeographic.org/resource/defining-battles-civil-war/

Why D-Day Matters
www.dday.org/learn/

About the Author

Marne Ventura is a children's book author and a former elementary school teacher. She holds a master's degree in education with an emphasis in reading and language development from the University of California.

Index

• Top Rank is an imprint of Black Rabbit Books. • Edited by Alissa Thielges | Designed by Danny Nanos • Photographs © Alamy Stock Photo/Shawshots, 30; Dreamstime/Houchi, cover, 1, Jiawangkun ,14, Kevin M. Mccarthy, 34–35; Library of Congress, 11, 22, Library of Congress/Carol M. Highsmith, 18–19, John Trumbull/N. Currier, 12–13, N. Currier, 14–15, Paris: Vve. Turgis, 16, Percy Moran, 17, 18; Shutterstock/Adam Parent, 25, adolf martinez soler, 37, Belinda Pretorius, 48, David W. Leindecker, 25, Domingo Saez, 2, 43, Everett Collection, 2–3, 21, 29, 32–33, 36, 37, 38–39, 40–41, 42, flysnowfly, 5, G Allen Penton, 20, JakeOwenPowell, 8, Jolygon, 46–47, Jorge Salcedo, 10, Karyl Miller, 26, Kumeko, 44–45, MattiaATH, 9, Mulley81587, 26, Shutterstock-Pixelsquid, 36, travelview, 17, Wirestock Creators, 6–7, woodsnorthphoto, 23; Wikimedia Commons/Currier & Ives, 27, John Trumbull, 9, Yale Center for British Art, Paul Mellon Collection/John Singleton Copley, 4, Mathew Benjamin Brady, 27, National Archives and Records Administration, 31, Seifert Gugler & Co., 28–29 • Printed in China

Library of Congress Cataloging-in-Publication Data Names: Ventura, Marne, author. | Title: 12 iconic American battles / by Marne Ventura. | Description: Mankato, MN: Black Rabbit Books, [2025] | Series: Iconic America | Includes bibliographical references and index. | Audience: Ages 9–13 | Grades 4–6 | Identifiers: LCCN 2024024630 | ISBN 9781645823926 (library binding) | ISBN 9781645824145 (paperback) | ISBN 9781645824367 (ebook) | Subjects: LCSH: United States—History, Military—Juvenile literature. | Battles—United States—Juvenile literature. | Classification: LCC E181 .V44 2025 | DDC 355.00973—dc23/eng/20240603 | LC record available at https://lccn.loc.gov/2024024630